BIBLE STUDY
Journal

Pebble
Edition

A brand of @rock.city.goods
rockcitygoods@gmail.com

Cover Design by @wildejoydesigns

Bible Study Journal and Bible Notebook | Bible Notebooks for Note Taking | Bible
Journal and Bible Study Notebook | Christian Journal for Women | Church Notes
Notebook and Bible Journal for Women | 8" X 10" Boho Notebook for Church

This Journal Belongs to

Date:

Scripture or Text

_____
_____

Notes and Observations

_____
_____
_____
_____
_____
_____
_____
_____
_____
_____
_____
_____
_____

Praise and Prayer

_____
_____
_____
_____

Date:

Scripture or Text

Notes and Observations

Praise and Prayer

Date:

Scripture or Text
_____
_____

Notes and Observations
_____
_____
_____
_____
_____
_____
_____
_____
_____
_____
_____
_____
_____
_____
_____

Praise and Prayer
_____
_____
_____
_____

Scripture or Text

_____

_____

Notes and Observations

_____

_____

_____

_____

_____

_____

_____

_____

_____

_____

_____

_____

_____

_____

_____

_____

_____

Praise and Prayer

_____

_____

_____

Date:

Scripture or Text

_____
_____
_____

Notes and Observations

_____
_____
_____
_____
_____
_____
_____
_____
_____
_____
_____
_____
_____
_____

Praise and Prayer

_____
_____
_____
_____

Date:

Scripture or Text

_____

_____

Notes and Observations

_____

_____

_____

_____

_____

_____

_____

_____

_____

_____

_____

_____

_____

_____

_____

_____

_____

_____

Praise and Prayer

_____

_____

_____

Scripture or Text

_____

_____

Notes and Observations

_____

_____

_____

_____

_____

_____

_____

_____

_____

_____

_____

_____

_____

_____

Praise and Prayer

_____

_____

_____

_____

Date:

Scripture or Text

_____

_____

Notes and Observations

_____

_____

_____

_____

_____

_____

_____

_____

_____

_____

_____

_____

_____

_____

_____

_____

_____

_____

Praise and Prayer

_____

_____

_____

_____

Date:

Scripture or Text

_____

_____

Notes and Observations

_____

_____

_____

_____

_____

_____

_____

_____

_____

_____

_____

_____

_____

Praise and Prayer

_____

_____

_____

Date:

<u>Scripture or Text</u>

<u>Notes and Observations</u>

<u>Praise and Prayer</u>

Date:

<u>Scripture or Text</u>

_____
_____

<u>Notes and Observations</u>

_____
_____
_____
_____
_____
_____
_____
_____
_____
_____
_____
_____
_____
_____
_____

<u>Praise and Prayer</u>

_____
_____
_____
_____

Date:

<u>Scripture or Text</u>

_____
_____

<u>Notes and Observations</u>

_____
_____
_____
_____
_____
_____
_____
_____
_____
_____
_____
_____
_____
_____
_____
_____
_____
_____

<u>Praise and Prayer</u>

_____
_____
_____
_____

Date:

Scripture or Text

_____
_____
_____

Notes and Observations

_____
_____
_____
_____
_____
_____
_____
_____
_____
_____
_____
_____
_____
_____

Praise and Prayer

_____
_____
_____
_____

Date:

Scripture or Text
_____
_____

Notes and Observations
_____
_____
_____
_____
_____
_____
_____
_____
_____
_____
_____
_____
_____
_____
_____
_____
_____

Praise and Prayer
_____
_____
_____
_____

Date:

Scripture or Text

_____
_____

Notes and Observations

_____
_____
_____
_____
_____
_____
_____
_____
_____
_____
_____
_____
_____

Praise and Prayer

_____
_____
_____
_____

Date:

Scripture or Text

Notes and Observations

Praise and Prayer

Date:

Scripture or Text

_____
_____

Notes and Observations

_____
_____
_____
_____
_____
_____
_____
_____
_____
_____
_____
_____
_____
_____

Praise and Prayer

_____
_____
_____

Date:

Scripture or Text
_____
_____

Notes and Observations
_____
_____
_____
_____
_____
_____
_____
_____
_____
_____
_____
_____
_____
_____
_____
_____
_____

Praise and Prayer
_____
_____
_____
_____

Date:

Scripture or Text

_____

_____

Notes and Observations

_____

_____

_____

_____

_____

_____

_____

_____

_____

_____

_____

_____

Praise and Prayer

_____

_____

_____

Date:

Scripture or Text

Notes and Observations

Praise and Prayer

Date:

Scripture or Text

_____

_____

Notes and Observations

_____

_____

_____

_____

_____

_____

_____

_____

_____

_____

_____

_____

_____

_____

Praise and Prayer

_____

_____

_____

Date:

Scripture or Text

Notes and Observations

Praise and Prayer

Date:

<u>Scripture or Text</u>

_____
_____

<u>Notes and Observations</u>

_____
_____
_____
_____
_____
_____
_____
_____
_____
_____
_____
_____
_____

<u>Praise and Prayer</u>

_____
_____
_____
_____

Date:

Scripture or Text

_____

_____

_____

Notes and Observations

_____

_____

_____

_____

_____

_____

_____

_____

_____

_____

_____

_____

_____

_____

_____

_____

_____

_____

Praise and Prayer

_____

_____

_____

_____

Scripture or Text

Notes and Observations

Praise and Prayer

Date:

Scripture or Text

_____

_____

Notes and Observations

_____

_____

_____

_____

_____

_____

_____

_____

_____

_____

_____

_____

_____

_____

_____

_____

_____

_____

_____

_____

Praise and Prayer

_____

_____

_____

_____

Date:

Scripture or Text
_____
_____

Notes and Observations
_____
_____
_____
_____
_____
_____
_____
_____
_____
_____
_____
_____
_____
_____

Praise and Prayer
_____
_____
_____
_____

Date:

Scripture or Text

_____
_____

Notes and Observations

_____
_____
_____
_____
_____
_____
_____
_____
_____
_____
_____
_____
_____
_____
_____
_____
_____
_____
_____

Praise and Prayer

_____
_____
_____

Date:

Scripture or Text

_____
_____

Notes and Observations

_____
_____
_____
_____
_____
_____
_____
_____
_____
_____
_____
_____
_____
_____

Praise and Prayer

_____
_____
_____
_____

Date:

Scripture or Text

_____
_____
_____

Notes and Observations

_____
_____
_____
_____
_____
_____
_____
_____
_____
_____
_____
_____
_____
_____
_____
_____
_____
_____
_____

Praise and Prayer

_____
_____
_____
_____

Date:

Scripture or Text

_____

_____

Notes and Observations

_____

_____

_____

_____

_____

_____

_____

_____

_____

_____

_____

_____

Praise and Prayer

_____

_____

_____

_____

Date:

Scripture or Text

_____
_____
_____

Notes and Observations

_____
_____
_____
_____
_____
_____
_____
_____
_____
_____
_____
_____
_____
_____
_____
_____
_____

Praise and Prayer

_____
_____
_____

Date:

Scripture or Text

_____

_____

Notes and Observations

_____

_____

_____

_____

_____

_____

_____

_____

_____

_____

_____

_____

Praise and Prayer

_____

_____

_____

Date:

Scripture or Text

_____
_____

Notes and Observations

_____
_____
_____
_____
_____
_____
_____
_____
_____
_____
_____
_____
_____
_____
_____
_____
_____

Praise and Prayer

_____
_____
_____

Scripture or Text

_____
_____

Notes and Observations

_____
_____
_____
_____
_____
_____
_____
_____
_____
_____
_____
_____
_____

Praise and Prayer

_____
_____
_____
_____

Date:

Scripture or Text

Notes and Observations

Praise and Prayer

Date:

Scripture or Text

_____

_____

Notes and Observations

_____

_____

_____

_____

_____

_____

_____

_____

_____

_____

_____

_____

_____

Praise and Prayer

_____

_____

_____

_____

Scripture or Text

Notes and Observations

Praise and Prayer

Scripture or Text

_____
_____
_____

Notes and Observations

_____
_____
_____
_____
_____
_____
_____
_____
_____
_____
_____
_____
_____

Praise and Prayer

_____
_____
_____
_____

Date:

Scripture or Text

_____

_____

Notes and Observations

_____

_____

_____

_____

_____

_____

_____

_____

_____

_____

_____

_____

_____

_____

_____

_____

Praise and Prayer

_____

_____

_____

Date:

Scripture or Text

_____
_____
_____

Notes and Observations

_____
_____
_____
_____
_____
_____
_____
_____
_____
_____
_____
_____
_____
_____

Praise and Prayer

_____
_____
_____
_____

Scripture or Text

_____

Notes and Observations

_____

_____

_____

_____

_____

_____

_____

_____

_____

_____

_____

_____

_____

Praise and Prayer

_____

_____

_____

Scripture or Text

_____
_____
_____

Notes and Observations

_____
_____
_____
_____
_____
_____
_____
_____
_____
_____
_____
_____
_____
_____

Praise and Prayer

_____
_____
_____
_____

Date:

Scripture or Text

Notes and Observations

Praise and Prayer

Date:

Scripture or Text

_____

_____

_____

Notes and Observations

_____

_____

_____

_____

_____

_____

_____

_____

_____

_____

_____

_____

_____

_____

_____

Praise and Prayer

_____

_____

_____

_____

Date:

Scripture or Text

Notes and Observations

Praise and Prayer

Scripture or Text

_____

_____

Notes and Observations

_____

_____

_____

_____

_____

_____

_____

_____

_____

_____

_____

_____

_____

Praise and Prayer

_____

_____

_____

Date:

Scripture or Text
_____
_____
_____

Notes and Observations
_____
_____
_____
_____
_____
_____
_____
_____
_____
_____
_____
_____
_____
_____
_____
_____

Praise and Prayer
_____
_____
_____

Date:

Scripture or Text
_____
_____

Notes and Observations
_____
_____
_____
_____
_____
_____
_____
_____
_____
_____
_____
_____
_____

Praise and Prayer
_____
_____
_____

Scripture or Text

_____
_____
_____

Notes and Observations

_____
_____
_____
_____
_____
_____
_____
_____
_____
_____
_____
_____
_____
_____
_____

Praise and Prayer

_____
_____
_____

Date:

Scripture or Text

_____

_____

Notes and Observations

_____

_____

_____

_____

_____

_____

_____

_____

_____

_____

_____

_____

_____

_____

Praise and Prayer

_____

_____

_____

_____

Date:

Scripture or Text
_____
_____
_____

Notes and Observations
_____
_____
_____
_____
_____
_____
_____
_____
_____
_____
_____
_____
_____
_____
_____
_____
_____
_____

Praise and Prayer
_____
_____
_____

Scripture or Text

_____

_____

Notes and Observations

_____

_____

_____

_____

_____

_____

_____

_____

_____

_____

_____

_____

_____

_____

Praise and Prayer

_____

_____

_____

Date:

Scripture or Text
_____
_____
_____

Notes and Observations
_____
_____
_____
_____
_____
_____
_____
_____
_____
_____
_____
_____
_____
_____
_____
_____
_____

Praise and Prayer
_____
_____
_____

Date:

Scripture or Text

Notes and Observations

Praise and Prayer

Date:

Scripture or Text

_____
_____
_____

Notes and Observations

_____
_____
_____
_____
_____
_____
_____
_____
_____
_____
_____
_____
_____
_____
_____
_____
_____

Praise and Prayer

_____
_____
_____

Date:

Scripture or Text

Notes and Observations

Praise and Prayer

Date:

Scripture or Text

_____

_____

Notes and Observations

_____

_____

_____

_____

_____

_____

_____

_____

_____

_____

_____

_____

_____

_____

_____

Praise and Prayer

_____

_____

_____

Scripture or Text

Notes and Observations

Praise and Prayer

Scripture or Text

_____

Notes and Observations

_____
_____
_____
_____
_____
_____
_____
_____
_____
_____
_____
_____
_____

Praise and Prayer

_____
_____
_____

Date:

Scripture or Text

_____
_____

Notes and Observations

_____
_____
_____
_____
_____
_____
_____
_____
_____
_____
_____
_____
_____
_____
_____

Praise and Prayer

_____
_____
_____
_____

Date:

Scripture or Text

Notes and Observations

Praise and Prayer

Date:

Scripture or Text

_____
_____
_____

Notes and Observations

_____
_____
_____
_____
_____
_____
_____
_____
_____
_____
_____
_____
_____
_____
_____

Praise and Prayer

_____
_____
_____
_____

Date:

<u>Scripture or Text</u>

<u>Notes and Observations</u>

<u>Praise and Prayer</u>

Date:

Scripture or Text

_____
_____

Notes and Observations

_____
_____
_____
_____
_____
_____
_____
_____
_____
_____
_____
_____
_____
_____
_____

Praise and Prayer

_____
_____
_____
_____

<u>Date:</u>

<u>Scripture or Text</u>

_____

_____

_____

<u>Notes and Observations</u>

_____

_____

_____

_____

_____

_____

_____

_____

_____

_____

_____

_____

_____

_____

_____

<u>Praise and Prayer</u>

_____

_____

_____

Scripture or Text

_____
_____
_____

Notes and Observations

_____
_____
_____
_____
_____
_____
_____
_____
_____
_____
_____
_____
_____
_____
_____

Praise and Prayer

_____
_____
_____
_____

Date:

Scripture or Text

_____
_____
_____

Notes and Observations

_____
_____
_____
_____
_____
_____
_____
_____
_____
_____
_____
_____
_____
_____
_____
_____
_____

Praise and Prayer

_____
_____
_____

Date:

Scripture or Text

_____
_____

Notes and Observations

_____
_____
_____
_____
_____
_____
_____
_____
_____
_____
_____
_____
_____
_____
_____
_____
_____

Praise and Prayer

_____
_____
_____
_____

Date:

Scripture or Text

_____

_____

Notes and Observations

_____

_____

_____

_____

_____

_____

_____

_____

_____

_____

_____

_____

_____

_____

Praise and Prayer

_____

_____

_____

<u>Date:</u>

<u>Scripture or Text</u>

_____

_____

<u>Notes and Observations</u>

_____

_____

_____

_____

_____

_____

_____

_____

_____

_____

_____

_____

_____

<u>Praise and Prayer</u>

_____

_____

_____

Date:

Scripture or Text

_____
_____

Notes and Observations

_____
_____
_____
_____
_____
_____
_____
_____
_____
_____
_____
_____
_____
_____
_____
_____
_____
_____

Praise and Prayer

_____
_____
_____
_____

Date:

Scripture or Text

_____
_____

Notes and Observations

_____
_____
_____
_____
_____
_____
_____
_____
_____
_____
_____
_____
_____
_____

Praise and Prayer

_____
_____
_____
_____

Date:

Scripture or Text

Notes and Observations

Praise and Prayer

Date:

Scripture or Text

_____

_____

Notes and Observations

_____

_____

_____

_____

_____

_____

_____

_____

_____

_____

_____

_____

_____

_____

Praise and Prayer

_____

_____

_____

Date:

Scripture or Text

_____

_____

_____

Notes and Observations

_____

_____

_____

_____

_____

_____

_____

_____

_____

_____

_____

_____

_____

_____

_____

_____

_____

Praise and Prayer

_____

_____

_____

_____

Scripture or Text

_____
_____
_____

Notes and Observations

_____
_____
_____
_____
_____
_____
_____
_____
_____
_____
_____
_____
_____
_____
_____
_____

Praise and Prayer

_____
_____
_____
_____

<u>Date:</u>

<u>Scripture or Text</u>

_____
_____

<u>Notes and Observations</u>

_____
_____
_____
_____
_____
_____
_____
_____
_____
_____
_____
_____
_____
_____
_____
_____
_____

<u>Praise and Prayer</u>

_____
_____
_____

Date:

Scripture or Text

_____
_____

Notes and Observations

_____
_____
_____
_____
_____
_____
_____
_____
_____
_____
_____
_____
_____
_____
_____

Praise and Prayer

_____
_____
_____
_____

Date:

Scripture or Text
_____
_____
_____

Notes and Observations
_____
_____
_____
_____
_____
_____
_____
_____
_____
_____
_____
_____
_____
_____
_____
_____
_____

Praise and Prayer
_____
_____
_____
_____

Scripture or Text

_____

_____

_____

Notes and Observations

_____

_____

_____

_____

_____

_____

_____

_____

_____

_____

_____

_____

_____

_____

Praise and Prayer

_____

_____

_____

_____

Date:

Scripture or Text
_____
_____
_____

Notes and Observations
_____
_____
_____
_____
_____
_____
_____
_____
_____
_____
_____
_____
_____
_____
_____
_____
_____
_____
_____

Praise and Prayer
_____
_____
_____
_____

Date:

Scripture or Text

_____
_____
_____

Notes and Observations

_____
_____
_____
_____
_____
_____
_____
_____
_____
_____
_____
_____
_____
_____
_____
_____
_____

Praise and Prayer

_____
_____
_____

Date:

Scripture or Text
_____
_____
_____

Notes and Observations
_____
_____
_____
_____
_____
_____
_____
_____
_____
_____
_____
_____
_____
_____
_____
_____

Praise and Prayer
_____
_____
_____
_____

Scripture or Text

_____
_____

Notes and Observations

_____
_____
_____
_____
_____
_____
_____
_____
_____
_____
_____
_____
_____
_____
_____

Praise and Prayer

_____
_____
_____

Date:

Scripture or Text

_____
_____
_____

Notes and Observations

_____
_____
_____
_____
_____
_____
_____
_____
_____
_____
_____
_____
_____
_____
_____
_____
_____

Praise and Prayer

_____
_____
_____

Date:

Scripture or Text

_____
_____

Notes and Observations

_____
_____
_____
_____
_____
_____
_____
_____
_____
_____
_____
_____
_____
_____
_____

Praise and Prayer

_____
_____
_____

Date:

Scripture or Text

_____
_____
_____

Notes and Observations

_____
_____
_____
_____
_____
_____
_____
_____
_____
_____
_____
_____
_____
_____
_____
_____
_____

Praise and Prayer

_____
_____
_____

Date:

Scripture or Text

_____
_____

Notes and Observations

_____
_____
_____
_____
_____
_____
_____
_____
_____
_____
_____
_____
_____
_____
_____

Praise and Prayer

_____
_____
_____

Date:

Scripture or Text

_____

_____

Notes and Observations

_____

_____

_____

_____

_____

_____

_____

_____

_____

_____

_____

_____

_____

_____

_____

_____

Praise and Prayer

_____

_____

_____

Date:

Scripture or Text

_____
_____

Notes and Observations

_____
_____
_____
_____
_____
_____
_____
_____
_____
_____
_____
_____
_____
_____
_____

Praise and Prayer

_____
_____
_____

Date:

Scripture or Text

_____
_____
_____

Notes and Observations

_____
_____
_____
_____
_____
_____
_____
_____
_____
_____
_____
_____
_____
_____
_____
_____
_____
_____

Praise and Prayer

_____
_____
_____
_____

Date:

Scripture or Text

_____

_____

Notes and Observations

_____

_____

_____

_____

_____

_____

_____

_____

_____

_____

_____

_____

_____

_____

_____

_____

Praise and Prayer

_____

_____

_____

Date:

Scripture or Text

Notes and Observations

Praise and Prayer

<u>Date:</u>

<u>Scripture or Text</u>

_____
_____

<u>Notes and Observations</u>

_____
_____
_____
_____
_____
_____
_____
_____
_____
_____
_____
_____
_____
_____
_____

<u>Praise and Prayer</u>

_____
_____
_____

Date:

<u>Scripture or Text</u>

_____

<u>Notes and Observations</u>

_____

<u>Praise and Prayer</u>

_____

Date:

Scripture or Text

_____
_____

Notes and Observations

_____
_____
_____
_____
_____
_____
_____
_____
_____
_____
_____
_____
_____
_____
_____

Praise and Prayer

_____
_____
_____
_____

Date:

Scripture or Text

_____

_____

_____

Notes and Observations

_____

_____

_____

_____

_____

_____

_____

_____

_____

_____

_____

_____

_____

_____

_____

_____

_____

Praise and Prayer

_____

_____

_____

_____

Date:

Scripture or Text

_____
_____

Notes and Observations

_____
_____
_____
_____
_____
_____
_____
_____
_____
_____
_____
_____
_____

Praise and Prayer

_____
_____
_____

Date:

Scripture or Text
_____
_____
_____

Notes and Observations
_____
_____
_____
_____
_____
_____
_____
_____
_____
_____
_____
_____
_____
_____
_____
_____

Praise and Prayer
_____
_____
_____
_____

Date:

Scripture or Text

_____

_____

Notes and Observations

_____

_____

_____

_____

_____

_____

_____

_____

_____

_____

_____

_____

_____

_____

Praise and Prayer

_____

_____

_____

Made in the USA
Columbia, SC
23 July 2022